Terrifying Tornadoes

Heinemann
LIBRARY

Louise and Richard Spilsbury

www.heinemann.co.uk/library
Visit our website to find out more information about **Heinemann Library** books.

To order:
 Phone 44 (0) 1865 888066
 Send a fax to 44 (0) 1865 314091
📠 Visit the Heinemann Bookshop at www.heinemann.co.uk/library to browse our catalogue and order online.

First published in Great Britain by Heinemann Library, Halley Court, Jordan Hill, Oxford OX2 8EJ, part of Harcourt Education.
Heinemann is a registered trademark of Harcourt Education Ltd.

Editorial: Andrew Farrow and Dan Nunn
Design: David Poole and Paul Myerscough
Illustrations: Geoff Ward
Picture Research: Rebecca Sodergren and Debra Weatherley
Production: Viv Hichens

Originated by Dot Gradations Limited
Printed in Hong Kong, China by Wing King Tong

ISBN 0 431 17837 2
08 07 06 05 04
10 9 8 7 6 5 4 3 2 1

British Library Cataloguing in Publication Data
Spilsbury, Richard, 1963 –
Terrifying tornadoes. – (Awesome forces of nature)
1. Tornadoes – Juvenile literature
I. Title II. Spilsbury, Louise
551.5′53
A full catalogue record for this book is available from the British Library.

Acknowledgements
The publishers would like to thank the following for permission to reproduce photographs:

AFP pp. **21** (Arko Datta-STR), **23** (Hector Mata-STF), **27** (Steve Schaefer-STR); Associated Press pp. **16** (Handout), **19** (Rahman), **20** (Carter), **26** (Schiappa); NOAA pp. **4**, **6**, **7**, **9**, **12**, **25**; Oxford Scientific Films pp. **15** (Faidley), **17** (Faidley); Photo Library p. **28** (Fema); Popperfoto p. **10** (Doherty); Rex Features pp. **5** (Houston Post), **14** (Houston Post); Science Photo Library p. **24** (Menzel).

Cover photograph reproduced courtesy of Getty Images/Taxi.

Every effort has been made to contact copyright holders of any material reproduced in this book. Any omissions will be rectified in subsequent printings if notice is given to the publishers.

Contents

What is a tornado?..................................... 4

What causes tornadoes?............................. 6

Where and when do tornadoes happen? 10

CASE STUDY: Tri-state Twisters, USA, 1925 13

What happens in a tornado?.......................... 14

CASE STUDY: Bangladesh, 1996....................... 18

Who helps after a tornado? 20

CASE STUDY: Oklahoma City, USA, 1999......... 22

Can tornadoes be predicted? 24

Can people prepare for tornadoes?.................... 26

Can tornadoes be prevented? 28

Terrifying tornadoes of the recent past 29

Glossary 30

Find out more 31

Index 32

*Any words appearing in the text in bold, **like this**, are explained in the Glossary.*

What is a tornado?

Tornadoes are among the most terrifying forces of nature. A tornado is a fast-moving, spinning column of air that twists down from a thundercloud. The twisting column of air reaches all the way down to the ground from the cloud in a **funnel**. Many tornadoes look like high, narrow black spinning tops. Other tornadoes look like incredibly long twisted ropes, or even bubbling masses of clouds.

Most of the tornadoes that happen are small. They may last for only a few seconds and do no damage at all. Large tornadoes can be hundreds of metres wide and kilometres high. These tornadoes are the most violent winds on Earth.

This is a picture of a typical tornado. Tornadoes are often called twisters, because of the way the winds within them twist and spin.

Tri-state Twisters, USA, 1925

The Tri-state Twisters were a terrible series of tornadoes that hit the USA on 18 March 1925. The tornadoes came in so close to the ground that people could not see them coming. They looked like big rolling clouds. The twisters raged through three states – Missouri, Indiana and Illinois – at over 100 kilometres per hour, following a ridge where many mining towns were built.

The Tri-state Twisters were very wide and brought terrible winds and heavy downpours of rain. They wrecked trees, farmland and buildings. They killed 695 people and injured over 2000. One town, Gorham, in Illinois, was totally destroyed and more than half of the population were killed or injured.

This map shows you the path of destruction followed by the Tri-state Twisters. This set of tornadoes was one of the worst in America's history. They lasted for three-and-a-half hours and finally broke up north-east of Princeton in Indiana.

What happens in a tornado?

People cannot always see the twisting tail of a tornado to tell them danger is on the way. Low storm clouds often hide approaching tornado storms. The first signs that a tornado is coming may be that the sky turns a dark green colour or big hailstones fall from the clouds. If you can hear a sound like a rushing waterfall or a roaring jet engine then the tornado is getting very close.

TORNADO FACTS

! A tornado moves like a spinning top. The winds in the **funnel** spin round and round at the same time as the tornado travels across a stretch of land.

! The winds in the funnel of a tornado can spin at speeds of over 500 kilometres per hour.

! A tornado can rush across the ground at up to 65 kilometres per hour, as fast as a moving car.

Some people think they can outrun tornadoes in their cars. But tornadoes can travel fast and they can toss cars about or roll them over and over as if they were toys.

How do tornado winds cause damage?

Tornado winds break things up and toss them around. Many of the people killed in tornadoes die when objects that are thrown through the air hit them. These winds can blow over walls, mobile homes, cars and trains and they can snap overhead cables and **power lines**, which can be very dangerous. Broken power lines can **electrocute** people or sparks from them may start fires.

The winds in the funnel of a tornado have incredibly powerful **suction**. Tornadoes can suck up anything, including millions of tonnes of dust, soil, sand or roof tiles. They drop them elsewhere when the tornado weakens. When soil and gravel are blown about by tornadoes they cause damage when people breathe them in or get them in their eyes. They can blow against things with such force that they act like sandpaper. They also clog up and **pollute** reservoirs and rivers.

Tornado winds move objects so fast that when they crash into something or someone they can cause serious harm. Even small objects, like this fork that has been embedded into a tree, can do a lot of damage.

Tornado strength

The strength of a tornado is judged by its wind speeds. Wind speeds are worked out from the amount of damage that they cause. It is too difficult and dangerous to measure them as they happen. The winds are often so strong that they destroy measuring equipment!

F-0 to F-1 tornadoes cause light to moderate damage to trees and buildings. They break off branches and knock down chimneys. They may also blow mobile homes over.

F-2 to F-3 tornadoes cause serious damage. They can tear the roofs off houses, lift and toss cars and overturn trains.

F-4 and F-5 tornadoes are the most violent winds on Earth. They can rip bark off trees, lift and carry whole buildings and throw cars over 100 metres! F-5 tornadoes usually occur only every other year in the USA.

The 'F' used to indicate tornado strengths stands for 'Fujita'. This is because the scale is named after the scientist who created it, Dr Tetsuya Fujita. Dr Fujita is pictured here, studying a mini-tornado created in his laboratory.

What is a tornado storm like?

The storms that produce tornadoes bring heavy showers of rain, thunder and lightning with them. Some have even dropped hailstones as big as tennis balls from the sky! Big hailstones like this can cause a lot of damage when they come crashing down to Earth.

When do tornadoes die?

Tornadoes usually break up when they go over colder ground or when the storm clouds above them break up. Most tornadoes only last about 20 minutes and travel less than 25 kilometres. However, some huge tornadoes have travelled 160 kilometres before dying.

Flying cows!

People have told stories of many strange things happening during tornadoes. Hens have had feathers plucked from their backs. Cows have been lifted up, mooing, and dropped down safely far away from their own field. One tornado lifted a pram high in the air and dropped it down again without waking the baby sleeping inside!

Imagine seeing huge hailstones like these falling from the sky towards you! These hailstones fell in Texas, USA.

Bangladesh, 1996

At lunchtime on 13 May 1996 in the Tangail district, north-western Bangladesh, the wind suddenly calmed and it got unbearably hot. Then hailstones the size of tennis balls fell from the sky as huge thunderstorms built up. These thunderstorms produced a series of terrible and destructive tornadoes. The tornadoes ripped bark from trees, uprooted large trees and caused many buildings to collapse.

Many people in Bangladesh are quite poor and their houses are not very strong. Many houses were built on hillsides out of reach of the floods that often happen during the **monsoon**, the country's wettest season. These houses were hit by the strongest winds.

'The whole village has been reduced to a vast grave.' A police officer in Bashail, one of the villages affected

This map shows where the tornadoes hit Bangladesh in May 1996. Bangladesh has about eight or nine tornadoes every year, usually in April and May, but the ones in 1996 were especially damaging.

Many people had built houses from thin sheets of metal. The tornado broke these up and threw the pieces about. The sharp metal pieces whirled in the air and injured many people. The bad weather and poor roads made it very difficult for rescuers to get to many of the villages. In some villages there were no trucks or buses. People had to carry injured friends and neighbours on their backs or in carts. Because of this, it was a long time before many injured people reached hospitals that could help them. By then their injuries had become infected and many died.

The tornadoes lasted about 2 hours and travelled over 25 kilometres. They left a path of destruction nearly 1.5 kilometres wide.

More than 80 villages and 10,000 homes were destroyed by the 1996 tornadoes in Bangladesh. More than 1000 people were killed and 30,000 people were injured.

Who helps after a tornado?

Imagine the scene after a tornado. Houses have collapsed and there is rubbish and **debris** strewn everywhere. Trees have been blown like matchsticks onto roads and buildings. The first people to arrive on a scene like this are rescue workers. They rescue people from cars, mobile homes and crushed houses.

Ambulances and medical workers arrive fast too. They give **first aid** to people who are injured and take those with more serious injuries straight to hospital. Some people will have dust in their eyes or throats which could make them ill. Flying debris may have injured others. Workers from **aid organizations** such as the Red Cross soon arrive. They provide people with the basics – food, clothing and **shelter**. They also provide food and drink to rescue workers.

Rescue workers may use their hands, spades, chainsaws or bulldozers to clear bits of wreckage to reach people who are trapped beneath it.

Finding loved ones

Aid organizations such as the Red Cross help people from other places find out if relatives in the tornado-hit area are safe and well. They also help families who were apart when the tornado hit to find each other again.

Clearing up

One of the biggest jobs after a tornado is clearing up the mess. Broken toys, furniture, clothing, fence posts, glass and crockery are strewn everywhere. Homeowners, **volunteers** and the Army or **National Guard** may all help. It can take weeks or months just to clear up the debris. When the rubble has been cleared, workers can mend or rebuild homes.

*When a tornado hits a **developing country**, people may not have enough money to rebuild their homes or businesses. As well as providing **aid** in the form of food and shelter, aid organizations may also supply tools or other equipment so that people can work and earn money again.*

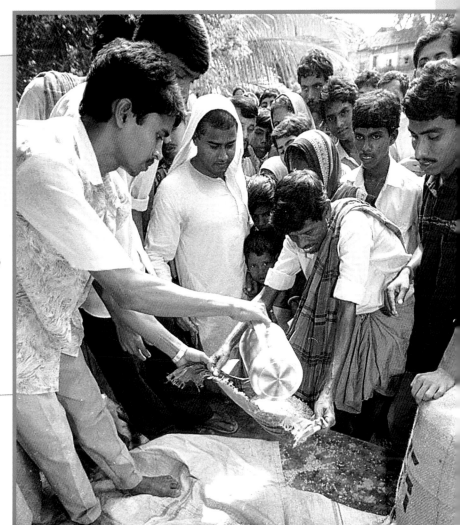

Oklahoma City, USA, 1999

In 1999, a tornado **swarm** ripped through the US states of Oklahoma and Kansas on Monday afternoon and Tuesday morning of 3–4 May. There were over 70 tornadoes in total. They raged across the land for over 4 hours. At least one of the tornadoes measured 1.5 kilometres across. Winds in some of the tornadoes blew faster than 300 kilometres per hour!

Cars and trucks were thrown around, trees and **power lines** were snapped and buildings were reduced to rubble. In Oklahoma City, an area called Moore was almost completely flattened. In total, thousands of houses were destroyed and 45 people were killed.

'It looks like a bomb hit here. Houses are just levelled [flattened]. It looks like a battlefield.' John Ireland, a resident of Moore

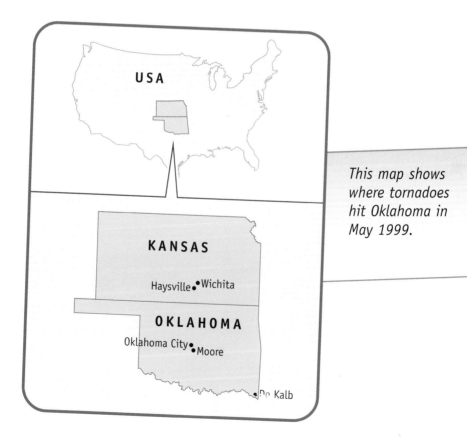

This map shows where tornadoes hit Oklahoma in May 1999.

Who helped in Oklahoma City?

Early TV and radio warnings meant that fewer people died in the disaster than would have been expected. However, many people still needed help. Rescue workers began searching the rubble for survivors straight away. They used dogs to sniff out where people were trapped. Then they used heavy machinery to lift away wrecked building parts. The American Red Cross set up **shelters** for people who had fled their homes or been rescued to spend the night in.

In the weeks after the tragedy, the government provided extra money to create temporary jobs for people whose factories or businesses had been destroyed. They also loaned money to many families so that they could afford to rebuild their homes.

*Hundreds of ordinary people gave money, tins of food, clothes and toiletry items (such as toothbrushes and towels) to an **aid fund**. This helped people who had lost their homes and all their belongings.*

Can tornadoes be predicted?

It is very hard to tell when a tornado will happen. Often, giant storms that seem likely to create a tornado do not, and small storms that do not usually produce a tornado do! However, scientists are working on ways of spotting tornadoes early so that they can warn people to get out of the way.

Weather reports

Weather forecasters can tell where storms are gathering and this helps to predict where tornadoes may start. They study pictures taken by **satellites** far above the Earth. These show where swirling clouds and thunderstorms are growing. They also get reports about storms from weather stations that operate in countries all over the world. In some countries there are groups of **volunteers** who watch out for tornadoes and phone weather stations as soon as they see signs of one.

Scientists use weather balloons like this to work out the direction and speed of the wind, high up in the air. This is one of the pieces of the puzzle they put together to work out when a tornado might happen.

Using advanced technology

Scientists use new technology as well as observing the weather to spot tornadoes early. **Doppler radar** is a special piece of equipment that can tell when there are strong spinning winds in a storm. These are the kinds of strong winds that might become a tornado. Scientists also use equipment that can **detect** lightning flashes between clouds even during daylight. They have worked out that faster flashing means a storm is getting worse.

Who are storm chasers?

Storm chasers are scientists who find and follow storms. They travel in vehicles with special equipment inside, such as video cameras and computers. They use this equipment to study how tornadoes behave. The information they collect is very useful for working out what to expect from future tornadoes.

Storm chasers try to get as close to the **funnel** of a tornado as they can in order to study it. It is dangerous work and they have to be very careful.

Can people prepare for tornadoes?

Only a small number of tornadoes actually hit people's homes every year, so it is very unlikely that even people in Tornado Alley will be affected. However, people who live in areas where tornadoes do happen can take steps to protect themselves.

Can buildings be made stronger?

People can make their buildings stronger and better able to resist tornadoes. They can bolt buildings to firm **foundations** and seal the gaps under roof tiles so winds cannot get underneath them. Many people build special **storm cellars**. These are either basements that are strengthened with concrete and strong doors, or separate rooms under the ground in the garden. People can hide in these during a tornado to be safe.

*This is a storm cellar. If people do not have a cellar like this, they should **shelter** in a room on the lowest floor of the house. They should keep away from windows and hide under something to protect themselves from flying **debris**.*

Tornado plans

People should not worry about tornadoes, but they should know what to do if one happens. In the USA, if a 'tornado watch' is announced it means that there is a possibility of a tornado and people should be ready to move to a safe shelter or **evacuate**. A 'tornado warning' means that a tornado has been spotted and people should run to their shelter immediately. Everyone in the family should learn exactly where to go and what to do.

Disaster supplies kit

People in tornado zones are also advised to prepare an emergency kit. This should contain:

- a **first-aid** kit
- a battery-powered radio (as electricity supplies may be cut off)
- a torch (and extra batteries)
- bottled water
- cans and packets of food (and a can opener!)

Local weather stations issue warnings about tornadoes. They send the warnings out as soon as they can on all radio and TV stations in the danger area.

Can tornadoes be prevented?

Tornadoes are natural forces that cannot be stopped. The only things people can do to reduce the damage tornadoes cause are to predict them earlier and be better prepared.

At the moment, only about half of all tornadoes can be spotted in time to warn people about them. In the future, scientists hope to set up systems across the world that can more accurately predict tornadoes. They are also working on ways to stop tornadoes forming. For example, people have tried firing **dry ice** into growing storms. The idea is to make the storm drop more rain, which makes it weaker. In this way scientists might be able to stop a storm producing any full-blown tornadoes.

*In order to reduce the amount of damage tornadoes can do, people need to understand what tornadoes are. This **volunteer** for the US organization **FEMA** is advising a local resident on what to do in the event of a tornado.*

Terrifying tornadoes of the recent past

4 January 1951, Comoro Island
The island of Comoro off eastern Africa was hit by a strong tornado. About 500 people were killed and the city of Anjouan was flattened.

19 April 1963, India and Bangladesh
A tornado travelling at 80 kilometres per hour touched down in India and passed through southern Bangladesh. In India, 139 people were killed and even more died in Bangladesh. People were picked up and thrown 300 to 600 metres.

Midwestern USA, 1965
On 11 April 1965, about 48 tornadoes crashed through the US states of Iowa, Wisconsin, Illinois, Michigan, Indiana and Ohio within a period of 12 hours. These tornadoes killed 256 people and caused more than $200 million of damage.

Dhaka, Bangladesh, 1969
Many people live in the city of Dhaka. When a tornado hit the city on 14 April 1969 it killed 50 people and injured 4000 more.

Midwestern USA, 1974
On 3 and 4 April 1974, 148 tornadoes raged for over 16 hours across the centre of the USA through thirteen states, including Ohio and Kansas. Over 330 people were killed and around 5500 people were injured.

Wichita Falls, Texas, USA, 1979
On 10 April 1979, three tornadoes killed 40 people and injured about 1700 more as they travelled across the US states of Texas and Oklahoma. Shopping **malls** and several hundred buildings were destroyed.

Midwestern USA, 1990
Around 50 tornadoes hit the midwestern USA within 4 hours. They killed 13 people and damaged 24 cities, within 7 states, from Wisconsin to Kansas.

Glossary

aid help given as money, medicine, food or other essential items

aid fund collection of money donated by ordinary people and used to provide aid

aid organizations groups of people who work together to raise money and to provide help for people in need

debris loose bits of solid material, such as stones and rocks

detect spot or find

developing country one of the poorer countries of the world that are gradually trying to develop better conditions for their people

Doppler radar special machine that uses invisible rays to detect where things are

dry ice frozen carbon dioxide. Carbon dioxide is a normal part of our earth's atmosphere. It is the gas that we exhale during breathing and the gas that plants use in photosynthesis.

electrocute kill by electric shock

evacuate when people move from a dangerous place to somewhere they will be safe

eye calm centre of a tornado (or hurricane)

FEMA stands for 'Federal Emergency Management Agency'. FEMA is an American government agency that is in charge of helping people before and after a disaster.

first aid first medical help given to injured people

foundations solid base upon which a building is built

funnel spiralling central part of a tornado

hurricane wind storms that are rather like tornadoes. Hurricanes are bigger and last longer than tornadoes and they start over warm oceans.

malls shopping centres

monsoon wet season in parts of Asia and elsewhere

National Guard volunteer soldiers recruited and trained by each US state. They serve during emergencies and in times of war.

pollute when part of the natural environment is poisoned or harmed by human activity

power lines main cables that carry electricity

satellite object that goes around the Earth in space. Satellites do jobs such as sending out TV signals or taking photographs.

shelter somewhere warm and safe to stay

storm cellar underground room where people can shelter during a bad storm, such as a tornado

suction sucking power
swarm group of tornadoes
tornado season time of the year when tornadoes happen most often
volunteers people who work without being paid for what they do

Find out more

Books

Wild Weather: Thunderstorm, Catherine Chambers (Heinemann Library, 2002)

DK Eyewitness Guides: Hurricane and Tornado, Jack Challoner (Dorling Kindersley, 2000)

DK Guide to Weather, Michael Allaby (Dorling Kindersley, 2000)

Storms, Mark Maslin (Hodder Children's Books, 2000)

Hurricanes and Tornadoes, Neil Morris (Crabtree Pub Co., 1998)

Websites

www.fema.gov/kids/tornado.htm – this website contains facts about tornado dangers, what to do and how to prepare.

www.nationalgeographic.com/eye/tornadoes/tornadoes.html – here you can see video reports from people who have lived through tornadoes.

Index

aid funds 23
aid organizations 20-1

Bangladesh 18-19, 29
breaking up 13, 17
building construction 26

causes of tornadoes 6

damage and destruction 5, 10, 12, 13, 14,
    15, 16, 18, 19, 20, 22, 29
deaths 11, 13, 15, 19, 22, 29
debris 20, 21, 26
developing countries 18-19, 21
disaster supplies kit 27
Doppler radar 25
dry ice 28

emergency aid 20-1
England 10
evacuation 27
eye of a tornado 8

F-scale 16
FEMA (Federal Emergency Management
    Agency) 28
funnels 4, 5, 6, 9, 14, 25

hailstones 14, 17, 18
hurricanes 7

location of tornadoes 10-11

monsoons 18
movement patterns 7

Oklahoma 22-3
outrunning tornadoes 14

pollution 15
power lines 15
predicting tornadoes 24-5
preparing for tornadoes 26-7
preventing tornadoes 28

recovery 21, 23
Red Cross 20, 21, 23
rescue workers 19, 20-1, 23
Rocky Mountains 11

satellite pictures 24
small tornadoes 4, 7
sound of a tornado 8, 14
storm cellars 26
storm chasers 25
storm clouds 8, 14, 24
strength of a tornado 16
suction 9, 15, 17
swarms 22

thunderstorms 17, 18, 24, 25, 28
timing of tornadoes 12
Tornado Alley 11, 12, 26
tornado seasons 12
tornado watch 27
Tri-state Twisters 13
twisters 4

USA 5, 10, 11, 12, 13, 22-3, 27, 28, 29

warm air 6, 11, 12
warning signs 14
warning systems 23, 24, 27
waterspouts 9
weather balloons 24
wind speeds 5, 6, 14, 16, 22
winds 5, 6, 7, 10, 14, 15

Titles in the *Awesome Forces of Nature* series include:

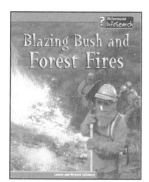

Hardback   0 431 17828 3

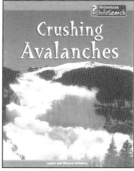

Hardback   0 431 17831 3

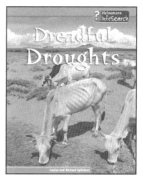

Hardback   0 431 17829 1

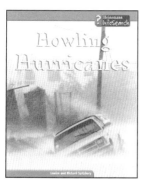

Hardback   0 431 17835 6

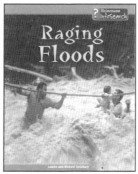

Hardback   0 431 17830 5

Hardback   0 431 17836 4

Hardback   0 431 17832 1

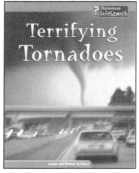

Hardback   0 431 17837 2

Hardback   0 431 17838 0

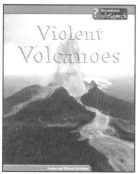

Hardback   0 431 17834 8

Find out about the other titles in this series on our website
www.heinemann.co.uk/library